PENGUII

Cheryl's L

Stephen Sexton's debut collection *I*   *were Young* won the Forward Prize for E   *collection* and was named 'a debut fit to compare to Seamus Heaney' (*Sunday Times*). He also received the E. M. Forster Award from the American Academy of Arts and Letters and the Rooney Prize for Irish Literature. He was the winner of the 2016 National Poetry Competition and the recipient of an ACES award from the Arts Council of Northern Ireland, and was awarded an Eric Gregory Award in 2018. He teaches at Queen's University, Belfast.

STEPHEN SEXTON

Cheryl's Destinies

PENGUIN BOOKS

PENGUIN BOOKS

UK | USA | Canada | Ireland | Australia
India | New Zealand | South Africa

Penguin Books is part of the Penguin Random House group of companies
whose addresses can be found at global.penguinrandomhouse.com

Penguin
Random House
UK

First published 2021
001

Set in 10/13.5pt Warnock Pro
Typeset by Jouve (UK), Milton Keynes
Printed and bound in Great Britain by Clays Ltd, Elcograf S.p.A.

The authorized representative in the EEA is Penguin Random House
Ireland, Morrison Chambers, 32 Nassau Street, Dublin D02 YH68

A CIP catalogue record for this book is available from the British Library

ISBN: 978–0–141–99752–0

www.greenpenguin.co.uk

for Bríd, walking through the forest

for it is walking through the forest

CONTENTS

PART III

Who are you going to believe, me or your own eyes?
The Marx Brothers, *Duck Soup*, 1933

The future is not immune from colonisation.
Ziauddin Sardar, *Future: All That Matters*

PART I

The Curfew

The radicals sprung the locks that night, hurrah!
and their lovely collarbones were almost moonly.

Rhinos shrieked and bellowed, elephants tromboned
and the animals nosed into town.

Sunrise to sunrise and sunrise we kept indoors.
If you can't count your onions, what can you count

my grandfather used to say. He said a lot of things.
Among the other miners he was legendary:

when no more than the thought of the pink crumple
of his infant daughter's body came to mind

a glow would swell in the pit, the men
would mayhem bauxite by the light

his tenderness emitted.
Some of me lived inside her even then.

The memorial fountain says nothing
of the weeks before the rescue failed

but mentions God which, as my grandfather
used to say, is just the name of the plateau

you view the consequences of your living from.
Or something like that. He said a lot of things.

He grew wise and weary as an albatross
and left for that great kingdom of nevertheless.

It would have pleased his handsome shoulders
to watch this grizzly scoop for salmon

in the fountain of his friends, or the Bengals,
or the shakedown squad of chimpanzees

who bang and bang on the grocery window.
One by one eleven miners starved to death.

In the streets they collar or tranquillise
the ocelots and run a spike of ketamine

through the plumbing in the fountain.
Dromedaries blue-mood around the pub

aloof under their reservoirs of fat.
I don't sleep, but oh plateau! these days

of violence have been my happiest.
Even a cabbage is not without desire

my grandfather said one day, and now
among the animals, I feel under my wings

the words for things I thought I knew
departing, and I understand him.

Segue

For the boys with the frog this is it.
No one mostly, older girls sometimes
pass on the straggle of back lanes,
for the birds what they talk about.
This variety of August
is untroubled surfaces, fields
of barley at the elbow
and within a stroll, a starve
of waste ground fly-tippers rust
their ancient engines on.
A boulder of liver-spotted granite,
a thumbprint on the belly of a frog.
Boys who carry ruin in their pockets
are becoming other people.

Samphire in the copper pan,
a splendour of salmon.
He's in traffic on the bridge
and this is years from then,
but cruelty is a time traveller.
It is paper, cotton, leather, doves,
the slope of Monte Carlo,
chanterelles, the Shangri-Las
the valley of the Rhône,
The Wichita Lineman
and its baritone guitar.
A knock at the door, she goes
and a one and a two and a
one two three four.

High School Musical

Milquetoast isn't the word – retiring,
diffident, wouldn't say boo to a goose.
However it happened, he was transformed:
six brass buttons on his double-breasted
prop naval officer's jacket glinted
in the stage lights and the boatswain's whistle
he brought to attention his children with
could be heard in this life and the next.

In those days I looked up to him, wooden,
kissing Maria not quite on the mouth.
In those days I was his right hand.
While he dumb-thumbed a Spanish guitar
and sang *Edelweiss* for the fatherland,
I hunched on a stool in the orchestra pit
and waltzed through the ache in my forearms.
Von Trapp fled Europe for America.

Mountains were unfastened and folded,
violinists slackened their bow hairs,
handshakes grew infrequent. After the show
I felt such an emptiness; I wanted
nebuchadnezzars of sweet Alsatian Riesling
to toast and swill with the Captain and crew,
but he was the sort for a prayer before bed
and a tick in the box marked *extracurricular*.

I expect he married and volunteered
for a mission in Zimbabwe or Chad,
and went on about water into wine
or the one about the wheat and the chaff,

until the miracles of nighttime and shame
brought twins each splendider than the other
and the big subpoena of the Lord
called him home to his native parish.

The last time I saw Daniel, a decade
thence, he was preaching brimstone
and worse from the bandstand
with a captain's steel and bearing.
I must be born again, Daniel, I know,
but wouldn't it be my luck
to be born into a golden age goldener
than the afterlife: so lovely, and so fucked.

My Second Favourite Locked Room Mystery

Since I started working at the bowling alley
I think about it all the time: in his barn
from a high rafter or crossbeam a man
has hanged himself with no ladder or platform
to get him there; nothing suspicious save
a patch of damp on the straw-strewn dirt floor.

Cheryl on the other hand is really into tarot.
When the soda fountain's not so busy
she shuffles up my destiny
and every time seems to draw THE LOVERS.
Think about it, flashes the braces in her smile
and the pinsetters chew like beautiful mouths.

Thinking about the future always makes me
so thirsty, so while Cheryl sorts out pin jams
and inventories the shoes, I slurp a Coke
with plenty of chipped ice and before long
my head is full of icemen and their cold chariots,
horse-drawn ice ploughs, the lakes of Massachusetts.

When she's fed up with kismet, Cheryl lets me
build little card castles, and I sometimes think
I could marry her some hot day in the summer:
an ice sculpture of a bowling pin undoing itself
into a puddle of water at the highest of June,
and I think of his horses, what were their names.

O Brother

I'm some pigeon, made by the same man
in shabby bus stations across the country:
Cork and Letterkenny; Derry and Dublin,
a few euros shy of the next departure.

Wherever he's going, there's his brother
in bad shape after a road traffic collision,
usually in A&E and unresponsive often
not expected to make it through the night.

What can I do but hear him out?
The café's closed today and for ever;
the coffee machine cappuccino
is a consommé of dust and hard water.

We're all past our glory.
A busted brother in every other city summons
someone to his deathbed to say sorry
for some upping of anchor and drifting apart.

But it's never abandonment, not quite,
just time's taking on a different music;
deltas, lemon groves, paddy fields, the world
framed by the windows of high-speed trains.

The second hand harries the hour hand:
buses glide like currency from the depot
where I fish in my pocket to offer this man
my sympathies, my smithereens of pelvis.

The Burdens

Before any of it, a goat appeared
in a piebald sweater, beardless
and tethered at the collar
on half a tennis court of land
up a rutted lane above the road.

Doubtless a horse once clip clopped there
before a trap, a whip, a tweed of farmer
with bushels and crates
of cabbages, parsnips, blue duck eggs
to pay the country doctor.

Not now, and not then,
we drive home between the fields.
She is radioactive, or lately was
and sleeps on the doses of nitrogen mustard
a country doctor has called for.

Little goat, forgive me. I shouldn't do this.
All you do is munch your poxy plain of grass,
your kingdom for a caper.
If at night you sing your tired chin to sleep,
it's not a metaphor, it's a tragedy.

Instead, let's say a ship arrived one day.
Let's say its decks were delicate, polished oak.
Let's say happy impossible winds steered it.
Let's say the captain, sweeping his spyglass
over the hills, after all this time, found us.

Marshalls of Saintfield

The battle done,
we'll see at last to the slow-puncture
needling the passenger side front tire.

So my father relates the happenings
of the parish: who in the nursery
raises copper beeches

doomed with cancer of the pancreas;
which handshake sold what field to whom
whereupon a fiction of sheep

negotiates grapeshot and bayonet
and chaws the world between
Saintfield and Ballynahinch.

It's the youngest son
who draws and tilts us off the earth.
A new liver couldn't save the eldest.

The old man with the middle distance
of sixty years of decibels and gesture
remembers Henry's yellow Austin, tut –

but it's a good thing to have, he tells me,
to work the words in the right order.
His youngest works the pneumatic jack.

A canter past the window of Marshalls,
tweeds and good, dark, smart suits.
I'd almost forgotten you were buried here.

Always the rumour
of double agents, of telegrams arriving
before what they describe has happened:

a family besieged with only thatch and fire
between themselves and poetry, and just
when they thought all hope was lost, it was.

On the double, Fencibles wheeled cannon
and marched in woolen redcoats and cross belts
to ambush, and days later, to victory.

So many years ago now, I agree, low
on the driver's side, with the radio's
inheritance of racing horses, and very.

Orthodox

When with his middle knuckle breaking rank
the boy jabbed me in the thigh,
the commerce of the playground trickled off:
the honky-tonker dove for cover,
the river buried its head in the card table.

A winter and the physique of trees so,
a morning of high rarefied air.
When he hit me he denied it:
no bruise, no strike.
He lit a match on his tongue, smoked cheroots.

If his shadow told it ten o'clock
across the chalk-white hopscotch boxes,
he denied his shadow.
If his fist went through a plate glass window,
the blood was someone else's.

Local dogs crooning, school bells.
The boyish lank of him went home I guess
or was expelled, or died.
How a bruise like a child blossoms
like nothing, look, a-ok.

You Don't Say

A gorgeous big lump of a horse of a bar
of English elm varnished with lightning
or lightning's recollection in the grain
electric still where the brigadier sits
in pinstripe and trilby and half-Windsor.
Who among us should wish him harm?

A bad sovereign frogs his little finger, yes;
a barman all nerves and adrenaline
walks like a bride with a posy of stout
to the end of the bar where the man holds court.
On the trophy shelf, an archer in bronze
never fires his arrow, and never misses.

We all have our affectations, Cheryl.
Most days, the bus takes me past the graveyard.
The graveyard is tender in its knowledge of us.
I feel you in my salts, says the graveyard.
Men alight and men embark before and after
flowers are replaced, and the plots left tidier.

Who among us should wish him harm?
He is generous in his society –
a companion, without fail, takes the first inch
from the top of his glass with a paper straw.
He's right to think the spies are everywhere.
They broadcast their dispatches from the grave.

O Lavery's

Dane Holt (6—6)

Of course, they must miss us like we miss them:
the spring-loaded cushions and rare vitesse
of table six, or table seventeen
of the cursed middle and top-right pockets,
or boys-a-dear, one scrappy afternoon
become a chalk-bewildered after-dark
sentineling the ward of table five
stuck for hours on free-play mode and sainted
where somebody with a physician's calm
draws under the supernatural light
the white across the otherworldly cloth
a shade of green my dreams can't reproduce;
who rolls their eyes and falls breathlessly to
the all-knowing bank of the possible.

Anniversary

The giddy cathedral swooned –
the night had been unremarkable for being remarkable
and was much like 1916 and mostly unlike the *Titanic*.
It would have been her twenty-fifth birthday, he said,
of the older sister he always felt had been his shadow;
who appeared in dreams as a porch light in the mist,
an igloo once, once as the breast plate and harness
of Dolph Lundgren as He-Man. The bars were closing.
Young men sallied in the streets like riderless horses.
She never had a name, he said, so he thought of one.

The avenue he lived on then reeled around a gigantic
horse chestnut tree, the pavement lousy
with conkers and seedcases. He said, you know,
everything in the world either is or isn't that tree.
Standing at the wrought iron railings, we recognised
a man we'd never seen before.
His distressed leather doctor's bag was handsome
and he opened it.

The Impossible

Beyond the canopy of oaks the path
we walk most evenings perseveres:
the medieval church holds out in ruins,
squirrels love their perpendicular lives,
a breeze brings news of the river
on the air
        and not exactly
the scrape of stonemasons at work
on the tombstone of our times
but an apprenticeship
of skateboarders chiseling
shivers of concrete from our civic spaces,
softening gently brutal edges, boys
and girls who bail nineteen times out of twenty
committed to impossible revolutions of the board
about both axes and fracturing a wrist
sometimes or an ankle past the walking off
of it and so lentissimo
paramedics cross the square.
And is it a muster of over-shirts,
a caravan of backpacks following
in the ambulance's wake
                or each alone
with gravity and the good new road
tarmacadamed smooth as time
downhill sooner than home and quick?
That's politics
however the good news is of the café bar
which not unlike everything is coming soon.

Afternoon at the Café Cependant

In the piazza of whatever
European city this is
fourteenth century
white marble arches
do their best to mutiny
against the season

curious breeds of dog
suffer the nuisances
of their genes
lapping ice water
clement waiters
splash into dishes

and there is no more joy here
than anywhere else.
Espresso cups
clink on their saucers
and the talk in English
is of the portraits

of x and x by so
and so and how once
a mother somewhere
loved that one
of the man standing
waist-deep in a river

his hat a skull
held out in his hand
waving so long

or hello my friend
the current is fine
and I am happy.

The sweet bitter blue smell
of matches
and cigar smoke
is on a breeze
someone prayed
to the gods of weather for

and the Coca Cola
someone said
she'd sell her soul for
is fizzing
in a high ball
on the table.

The rickety waltz
an accordion wheezes
mesmerises no one;
a gypsy jazz
guitarist catching
the likeness

of his father's face
in his own reflection,
drops the beat
and blushes and laughs.
Cousins you imagine
kiss each other

on the cheeks across
the square. A husband
in a bistro sweats,
chiffonades and juliennes,
yes, he says to the celery
my marriage is over.

Later the thunderstorm
throws its weight around
and only the statues remain
in the bronze of their poses
dreaming of
the opposite of and.

It will be a long night
says Pierre to the peppermill
in the pale light
the generator rations out,
poaching excellent pears
in honey and moscato:

the masterstroke
of another great banquet
no one living is invited to.
So what he says
to the no one
he loves.

Romantic

It's hard to mourn in shorts, a straw hat, flip-flops.
Cats from the sanctuary sunbathe nude
on the headstones, or cool the embassies
of themselves among the pomegranate trees.

Would the cicadas ever quit buckling their ribs.
A gecko goes bouldering over Antonio Gramsci's grave
and the beautiful teeth of American tourists are sparkling
but they can't help it, and we are tourists too.

We drink water by the jeroboam
and go over again the terrible things Percy Shelley did
in the name of his fireproof heart.
Die by drowning or don't – these remain our options.

The water cycle magics on like something
finer than a clock and John Keats
it's nice to meet you, under the circumstances.
And John Keats, please excuse us, time has made it late.

It's today already
and we have only the rest of our lives.
Long may we dabble our feet in the clear Italian lakes.
Long may we mosey through the graveyards of the world.

PART II

On the afternoon of October 24th 1917, four days after my marriage, my wife surprised me by attempting automatic writing. What came in disjointed sentences, in almost illegible writing, was so exciting, sometimes so profound, that I persuaded her to give an hour or two day after day to the unknown writer, and after some half-dozen such hours offered to spend what remained of life explaining and piecing together those scattered sentences. 'No,' was the answer, 'we have come to give you metaphors for poetry.'

W.B. Yeats, 'Introduction to "A Vision"', from *A Packet for Ezra Pound* (1937)

On the afternoon of March 20th, 2020 – the spring equinox – a deep drowse. Over the course of the day and night, these poems were communicated to me by an unknown presence.

Strange times says everyone from their TOWER
communing daily with nobody else.

In the image of spring and through the glass
a crisis of crocuses burgeons on.

In Georgia, almost thirty years ago
Billy Corgan of The Smashing Pumpkins

on his own in the studio tosses
scrunched-up paper at the waste-paper bin.

I read the works of W. B. Yeats,
doze, and play *Siamese Dream* on repeat.

They say you are the company you keep.
William Butler Yeats and Billy Corgan;

Gemini and Pisces are, according
to auguries, incompatible signs.

Siamese Dream
for the Cloths of Heaven:

A Collaboration

4:58

Is this heaven, says W. B. Yeats.
Virtually, says Billy, this is Georgia.

So, here is Yeats in 1992
suddenly at the recording sessions,

body and spirit split at last between
marriage in middle age and Atlanta.

Whatever his take on shoegaze, dream pop
or the whole phenomenon of 90s

alternative rock, having no passion
for Elvis Presley even, no one knows,

but wherever he's summoned he must go.
                  Who wants honey, says Yeats, to break the ice,

I have there a hive for the honeybee.
        That's it, screeches Billy, that's the chorus!

Like everything that has the stain of blood,
                we must remember beyond his making

                the drummer cut takes until his hands bled
                to Billy himself mad-scientising

                with the great wheels of the amplifier,
                but what a tender brute with the guitar:

the bell that calls us on; the sweet far thing,
the horn's sweet note and the tooth of the hound.

                        Quiet, I am sleeping in here, Billy,
and hear amid the garden's nightly peace,

the night has fallen; not a sound, says Yeats.
                And so their collaboration begins,

                each at the elbow of his century,
                tenors singing in search of their burning vehicles.

3:19

'The Great Day' is a gift Yeats will treasure,
so great a glory did the song confer,

all hurt and wonder in E-flat major,
the sentimentalist of all the keys.

The beggars have changed places, but the lash
goes on, Yeats is singing sotto voce,

the sentimentalist himself; while art
is but a vision of reality.

[2:03–2:06], says Billy.
He may have banished the band in a rage

but with Yeats' expertise he's destined
to wrap the album growing overdue.

I'll burn my eyes out before I get out
the majesty that shuts his burning eye.

6:57

W.B. Yeats is stone-cold tone deaf.
He won't know the imperfect consonance

of a lovely major third in his ear;
the ground dizzy with harmonious sound

of the humming sands and the humming sea,
the dense music of an apiary

buzzing with the drones of work and honey.
Billy's saying it's a beautiful song,

a coda winding towards its target;
a feather floating towards its cadence:

it scares the disenchanted far away.
It was the dream itself enchanted me,

says Yeats, winding guitar cables cubit
by palm like an eager junior cadet.

4:06

What in the name of who knows what is this?
An unseen hand guides mine, what can I say

but seek alone to hear the strange things said.
These days indoors demand one make one's art

from whatever the imagination
can manage to blend together, and yet,

what shall I do with this absurdity:
a crown of horns, an image formed deformed.

Till meditation master all its parts,
and under Yeats' direction, they work late

polishing the demos, implicating
vast chains of delay, echo and chorus.

I saw my freedom won, Billy repeats
to the man who can teach him how to praise.

3:17

Wartime salute, Billy: an anagram
                          inside of me and such a part of you.

Yeats is talking about 1918:
my heart would brim with dreams about the times.

We had to get away from it, Billy,
me and Georgie were bored out of our minds,

and she's so impatient for the future;
half the time she's a century away.

                    The bitterness of one who's left alone,
says Billy, and Yeats agrees, and goes on:

surely there are men who have made their art
out of no tragic war, lovers of life,

impulsive men that look for happiness,
they seemed to sing in the smouldering fires.

6:39

We're like a pair of soma-drinking priests!
      Billy's drawn something glowing and high-proof

      from his purple-velvet-lined guitar case.
This night can set us quarrelling, Billy!

        about the body, the spirit, the soul,
        and which is which and who is whom and where,

        and Billy says, hey Yeats, would you shut up
        for a tick, conjuring a cadenza

so virtuosic the perning world stops.
O saddest harp in all the world, says Yeats,

        dabbing at his eyes next to the tape reels.
O kinsmen, bless the hands that play, he says.

                To anyone caught in our ruse of fools,
but the escape; the song's not finished yet.

5:13

Retrospect connects us, Billy, says Yeats,
Siamese twins at the wrist, and then I

most like me, being indeed my double,
had half awakened some old memory —

Why don't we let them talk this out, Georgie?
I don't know about you, these days it feels

like all of history happens all at once
and the impulse is irresistible

to metaphor the moment just because,
to know it as something beyond itself.

As one hand knows another taking it,
now nothing but comes readier to the hand;

it's up to someone else to make us mean.
I feel their thumbprints warming our margins.

5:50

I think we've broken the back of it now,
says Billy, between toothaches of feedback

whistling through the $60 guitar
whenever he takes his hand off the strings,

a racket rankling Yeats' nerves no end.
He's having none of the whole idea

failure or fault might be the essential
motivation for any piece of art.

When my hand passed from wire to wire
it quenched, with sound like falling dew, says Yeats.

[1:32–1:36], Billy
says to a man whom Sorrow named his Friend.

I'm rumoured to the straight and narrow, Yeats,
those terrible implacable straight lines.

4.28

Spaceboy, I've missed you spinning round my head
on that unfashionable gyre again.

At this stage of the night everything goes
giddy, inches towards the witching hour.

What is there but the slowly fading west,
the brilliant moon and all the milky sky.

Yeats raises a toast with an empty glass:
when we are dead, beyond the setting suns,

a little from the other shades apart,
those dying generations at their song —

Yeats, will you sing harmony on this one?
And I that made like music in my youth?

We'd drink a can or two, Billy, says Yeats,
a rapturous music, till the morning break.

8:43

This is what we would call a dream vision.
Yes, but who is imagining who, Yeats?

Delight makes all of the one mind, says Yeats.
You have your songs and I mine, says Billy,

but what's the metaphor you're looking for?
A metaphor is only a person

trying very hard to be understood
at the edge of their imagination.

I know I've been a dick to the band, Yeats.
I haven't been myself for years, Billy.

Perfection of the life or of the work.
I hear your winter and I hear your rain

through summer's heat and winter's cold, Billy,
POETRY, music, I have loved, and yet —

Is it all done with computers, Billy?
Yeats is asking, fidgeting with his watch.

By hand: the producer takes a razor
to the tape and splices it in sequence.

Cut out our rhymes on strips of new-torn bark!
It's got to be a lot of work, Billy?

It's years, Yeats, and they all want you to change.
And you have changed and flowed from shape to shape?

I'm too old to change, Yeats, I'm twenty-five.
Georgie's about your age, and she changed me:

dutiful husband, honest wife by turn.
And where is this honest wife of yours, Yeats,

half in the past or half in the future?
She sings as the moon sings: I am I am.

I'll sing for you, if you want me to, Yeats.
Sing me the changes of the moon once more.

from the first crescent to the half, the dream
found certainty upon the dreaming air.

I'm certain I'm certain of nothing, Yeats,
Whatever I dream, whoever dreams me

across the long night of a century.
Of the old world on dreaming fed, Billy.

We're neither the old world nor the new world,
nor even the moment those worlds turn on

but dreams that hurry from beyond the world;
the loop of tape between the reel-to-reels

written, rewritten and overwritten
over there in recorded history.

Strange times says everyone from their TOWER
over there in recorded history

half in the past or half in the future
Virtually, says Billy, this is Georgia

the drummer cut takes until his hands bled
I hear your winter and I hear your rain

Yeats, will you sing harmony on this one
the sentimentalist of all the keys

the dense music of an apiary
it quenched, with sound like falling dew, says Yeats

to metaphor the moment just because
can manage to blend together, and yet

and she's so impatient for the future
for a tick, conjuring a cadenza

PART III

A Pledge

I say let's not fell a sequoia
or any other huge and ancient tree
and chisel out a bungalow to live in.
Sweetheart, amigo, it would take forever.

We're not lumberjacks or surgeons
or carpenter ants or blizzards or today, anyway
death galloping through the woods
in the black dress of a wildfire.

Yes, each dead bird is one
in the allness of birds
but such a tree is a mortgage
of sawdust and sap

and suppose he's elderly:
the man dying in his parlour
in the body a skeleton
floats to the surface of?

If the sound of chopping wood
is on the air, holy men say
the soul cannot escape
and agony, agony, but even

the unsuperstitious are suffering
on Tuesdays or Thursdays
acutely in bedrooms
near scarecrows or not near them.

Is it moral to abstract oneself
from someone else's suffering
or the opposite? The answer
bolts like Fido from his master

and will not heel. And besides
it's passé: living in the woods
with its dreamboat night sky
and its fragrant respiration

and and and and and and and
you might say, excuses.
And were it not for the cherish
of your hi-vis and hardhat;

the promise of your axe in the air,
I'd have said let's not and meant it
and swung no such almighty cut
into our luxury mausoleum.

MYSTERIES
Orthodox

i.m. L.B.

It makes none of me happy
to think the fierce plum of his fist, even,
will not unfurl and busy itself again
against my breastbone or plummet

of ribs and him still boyish
(if new seas are between him and school bells)
and dead at this age: the circuit breaker
faulty; rage or whatever general and only.

I think always of the alien body-brain
of the octopus, whose thoughts
are in its arms, whose self-destructions
are slow and commonplace as tides;

how should it abrade and sever an arm
the arm will frolic and prey beyond itself
and return far too late subsistence
to wherever the mantle floats and doesn't.

MYSTERIES
Two Loughs

i.m. Cat McCrory

Introduced for the fifteenth time in ten years
we shook hands one night outside Voodoo

or The Duke of York or Lavery's
and since promises tell the future, vowed

from now on, to know each other by name.
The glasses of beer wouldn't drink themselves.

At the megalithic tomb at Carrowkeel
a wrong turn is a shriek of agile sheep

who scatter and leap the dry stone walls.
In bed somewhere someone imagines this.

A path more stony pilgrimage than desire:
horseflies, heather, banks of yellow hair grass;

Beyond Arrow, Lough Gill miles away in the sun
like a bowl of mercury;

an itinerary of weeping; but you know this—
wounded with all knowledge as you are now.

Word comes unfalteringly over these hills
and finds me deer-footed in espadrilles

and stops me here, above the tesselate fields,
the islands floating in the lough

named for her who was called bright
and to whom every harbour was known.

MYSTERIES
Terrestrials

i.m. Lukasz Karpinski

A sparrow weaves over the derelict terrace
the psychics used to meet in

towards the snow-garnished mountains!
They brought their lozenges of grief here,

held each other's pallid hands and summoned
reeds of kindness into their voices!

The men down tools, take lunch, smoke
in a row, dangle their legs from the wall!

They're kids mostly; a xylophone
of hard hats tuneless in the rain!

The half-built apartment block is waiting
and they will never live there!

I knew a boy who wanted to be a pilot
so much that he became one!

Farewell, years of simulated taxiing
on the world's fantastic runways!

O night flights over the patchwork of Europe!
O unscheduled layover! O seat belt sign!

I knew a man who hiked into the mountains!
His name was early morning light!

His name was sunset in Libra!
Between the Scots pine and the Ash

he found the branch with his name on it
and stepped off it into the air!

*

I was thinking about dinosaurs and drinking beer
in Denver when I heard the news!

The beer was lovely, cold and tart,
the bones were very buried in the planet!

A few aspirin, goodnight!
The man was carried down from the mountains!

His name was a rhetorical question
the hustle of elegy is no answer to!

I ought to telephone my father!
I ought to mend this flapping epaulette!

I ought to teach my tongue not to cut itself
on the new edge of an old tooth!

I ought to pour us each a toast of beer,
and get back to work on the fan fiction!

Phew! Yuri said, as the engine sputtered to a stop,
That was a close one!

Valentina smiled and a breeze took her hair!
She thought, Let us live for a long time!

And the great spaceman climbed down
from the cockpit and walked towards her!

There she was on Planet Earth!
On the good Earth they took each other's hands!

For Gomez

it's waltzes, lovemaking and DEATH
in the mansion by the graveyard
whose mansard roof's cascading slates
are forces majeures of guillotine

and wrought iron gates wanting oil
are spiked with poignards élégants
where a sentry pair of magpies
is nothing more than sorrow twice.

Knowing here, you know hereafter
is the smoulder of Armagnac,
cigars and a smoking jacket,
an odd aristocratic bent;

the old country's romantic tongues,
marriage's drawn-out ecstasy:
there's nothing of oblivion
even cousinly to surprise.

Neither the bats in the belfries
of Castille nor the endless bilk
of the new world's grand prospectus:
Death is the rightful republic.

What we could learn from you, old man,
in the callithump of living
is to refuse to be subject
to opposing jurisdictions;

to love the house where suffering
is not suffering desire,
whose gates swing open at a thought:
we should never have been strangers.

Humour

It's nothing, he would say,
crying at the burger joint.
Not the malt in the milkshakes
nor the tint of iron in the beef
not Mercury in retrograde
not the office job, not the price
of gold or crude, not Cheryl
receding lately into herself
like a little sailboat unmoored
drifting on the great moony sea.

In wet yellow mackintoshes
kids arrive like emissaries
and the future keeps happening
to them. And it's true there was
nothing, as far as he could tell,
that had him cry in the burger joint.
Nevertheless, tears fell in his lap
mysterious and many
as the sesame seeds dashed
in the bun of his cheeseburger.

The Chair

The old Hitachi dual cassette was pain
and elegant with age, and the branches were,
and the sash window was open with pain,
and the afternoon was adequate, and pain.

Children roller-skating in the street were pain
and the hum of the imminent sunset was.
Would I say today was, and all today's heirs?
Yes, I would bet tomorrow morning on it.

My mouth these many years was wealthy with pain.
For so many years, I thought *prodigal* meant
destined to return transformed and beloved.
The dentist doesn't ask me where I've been.

I'm tired of the war, I wanted to say,
but my jaw fell slack, so he buried the nerve,
finding in his caulking gun of composite
the inverse of a tooth, the way a good eye

can find intemperate horses galloping
within a block of marble. Then the x-rays.
I've been setting off supermarket alarms
lately, I wanted to say, to tell someone.

Whose are the dreams I'm having? I'm never there
on the balcony, with free jazz and treason.
Then the pain was replaced with its memory,
which is to say that nothing ever changes.

He left. The hygienist grew ungenerous
with silence. I rinsed with something glowing green.
You know she talks about you sometimes? she said.
        Who does? I said.

The Messages

On Sunday afternoons the price of broccoli
may well drop by eighty percent,
the noodles bear the pallor of the travel sick,
but the uncontracted can't be picky

though the troubled, otherworldly stare of hunger
only adds to the spooky aesthetic
lazy or at-their-wits'-end detectives expect
from their local psychic correspondent;

should the missing person remain undiscovered
in the abandoned trophy factory
and the only recourse be supernatural,
it's Cheryl who is waiting by the phone.

Hers is a dying trade—there's no future in it,
she'd say—but a gift wasted is a sin,
however hard it is raising handfuls of boys
on a couple of hours of work a month

and Agony-Aunting for glossy magazines,
but harder is catching the cashier's eye
and not seeing the routine mysteries of love
and divorce, but a moonlit winter's night

a multi-story car park a decade away,
from somewhere, a flash of bristling rage,
and knowing the boys will be teenagers by then
or were already, or never won't be.

An Act of Going

New geometries
of brilliant aluminium

a few pristine helmets
the boys of Christmas morning

pedal along the quay
a loose braid of dazzling oaths

big talk and cigarettes
for now the town is theirs

the universe for all they know
keeps the lights on for them.

No hands is elementary
but show-stopping

is two boys drawn parallel
uncrossing their arms

and by fingertip by palm
each taking the other's hand

however costly to balance
however alien the intimacy

and coming to grief
laughing on the cobblestones.

Across the river in which
teenagers drown themselves most months

the half-built Ferris wheel
is the nervous system of the moon.

Wind shears off the water
through intricacies of spoke

and yes, boys, always yes
someone should be watching

and I am your mothers,
but oh how the flag whips the flagpole.

The Green Rooms

Because the human eye can see
so many shades of green,
the couple filled their modest flat
with ferns and Parlour Palms

and aspidistra, and aloes,
a Baby Donkey's Tail,
two weeping figs, a desert rose,
some fishbone cactuses.

To call in on them is to breathe
what forests sing about—
a chorus of viridian.
I do some Sunday nights,

for Beaujolais and company
and dozing off, the plants
say the kinds of things children might,
but they are not children.

The Dancers

All the syrup-lighted afternoon I watch the office block
Be dismantled into discretions: half-moon desks
Rolled like a fibreboard month across the gummy carpet,
The clank and tango of a filing cabinet impressed
By three stout men towards the backmost stairwell
Where the line of people standing one abreast
Snakes throughout the building's seven floors.
I water the feeble mint and the oregano flowers
And the hyacinths in the shade of my balcony
And the whippings start up again in the street below.

On a bus somewhere, or a train, you come towards me
And the second-generation children singing pop songs
On the mezzanine, approximating the dance routines,
Whose fortunes of language they cannot cherish yet.
You'll say I've never felt such uncomplicated joy
And we'll stand there in the hall with your suitcases
Listening to whatever rendition, whatever song
And you'll say what a thing to share this flake of time
In their company, what a thing wild lavender
Can still flourish in the grounds of the derelict church.

A Short History of Happiness

In a red desert
someone's last pure thought
invents the heaven she has no name for
the heaven we call a water tap
so unimaginable as to be beyond
a miracle fifty generations away
a hundred, a thousand
and she passes uncredited
almost out of history,
where history is what we call
what might have happened differently
and didn't, such as
a good man's joy this spring morning
in his lovely office polished free
of breath and fingerprints, even his
waste-paper basket emptied somehow
where the magic amaryllis
despite his never watering it
shows new, majestic, red flowers.

from The Beasley Contract Bridge System, *1935*

Notice the gaps in the various suits.

Imagine your partner with nothing at all.

You retain for your partner or yourself all the possible loopholes
　　　of escape.

That is safety and precision—not chance.

For here again the story of the hand must be told:
　　　(a) I have nothing
　　　(b) I have something, not a lot
　　　(c) I have a great deal.

You can check what I say.

There will be cases of duplicated values, there will be cases of
　　　freakish adverse distribution.

You can check what I say.

I do not propose to waste your time by criticising other systems.

Too many, however, are based upon what to do with big hands,
　　　and forget that the majority of hands dealt are ordinary.

We spent the time on the boat perfecting him in the system.

I offered to tell him how many tricks could be made on the hands.

We brought back the trophy.

Consistent profit is far more satisfactory than an occasional excitement.

That may be considered American, but it has now become internationally general.

There is no game in sight. We are in danger.

Here you have the Principle of Security hard at work.

This will nullify the effect of a psychic double.

Then the hands will go wrong.

It may seem a strange procedure to talk about hands that are not No Trumps before dealing with those that are. But this is exactly the mistake commonly made.

Each bid not only tells the strength of the hand, it tells this plain truth.

There is no game in sight. We are in danger.

It may seem that you are legislating for an infrequent happening.

The opposition are most likely to bid.

It may seem that you are legislating for an infrequent happening.

Vulnerable or not, that is a justifiable sacrifice.

You can check what I say.

"I have taken your bid at minimum and added my maximum, and
    together we can get so many tricks."

Psychology is important, but no book can deal with that.

The opposition are most likely to bid and they have no idea of
    your strength.

Terror

First arrived a pair of antique broadswords
passed point to pommel through the letterbox
in a jute sack, with no return address.
Lancelot, Melion, Galahad, O
all the knights we know are dead.

We changed light bulbs all morning,
unpacked books, bled radiators.
Albert on the lawn introduced himself
to each of the daffodils and we began to live there
and Scorpio slipped into Sagittarius.

Some daggers made from cassowary bone
came bubble-wrapped, and anthropologists
of some renown determined their origin
to be Papua New Guinea, mid-18th century.
Housewarming gifts, we told little Albert.

Though we loved the moon, the moon
could not defend us, loving as it does the sea.
For weeks we slept like avocados.
An avocado is its own unit of time, we thought,
goosebumped and spoiling in our bedroom.

Had we known the werewolves were so many
we would not have come, my wife said to Albert.
He loves werewolves the way terror has an opposite.
They cannot themselves be responsible
for what night does, she said.

Letters came floating by with directions
to anywhere else but our cul-de-sac
in the heebie-jeebie script of werewolves;
then came the trebuchet, flat-packed,
assembled in the garden one afternoon.

The Kamov Ka-60 Kasatka landed complete
with two Russian pilots, both milk and two sugars.
They missed their families, the steppes, the snow.
St. Petersburg has its charms, said Sasha.
Red Square is quite beyond compare, replied Sasha.

An orca, Esmeralda, belly-flopped on the lawn
next to the helicopter, clicking curses
like a massive handbrake. For Albert we left.
The world still has a big soft place for him
so we packed our things and set out for it.

So long daffodils, see ya sunflowers!
He'll grow up to be kind as the daylight
some tomorrow morning the people
stand naked in their mirrors
saying I'm sorry, for everything, I'm sorry.

Street Fighter II

The Laxey waterwheel, or Lady Isabella, shoots the breeze
with batteries of tailless cats who linger by the silver mine.

I'm in a dim basement arcade somewhere once in Douglas
        palming
ten ten pence pieces into Ryu's disciplined and storied fists.

So to a village of cinchona, the Brazilian Amazon
where a yellow anaconda constricts a mahogany tree;

so to a bright sumo dojo in Honshu where the sun happens
perpetually to rise near the symmetrical peak of Fuji;

so to the cascade of salt which is the promenade where I see
the first and last time, by dint of gin and tonics, my mother
        drunk;

an impression of an eight-year-old falls into the Irish sea.
In those days of the promenade the sun still swung from east to
        west

and don't doubt for a second the moon then looked almost
        exactly
like it does to you now: like melted bone, like something's severed
        limb.

In the airforce base at Langley an F16 had dipped its beak
In the oil fires of Kuwait and it's Major Guile and his flash kick

I just can't seem to beat—he's more leg than man, more man than
      pixel.
Had I seen then the black mirage of the future, I might have
      thought,

wouldn't it be fine to climb into the machine and carry on
like the automated Turk, going down, down-forward, forward;

had my life glitched just then, I might have swapped my bones
      for PCBs
and said bring your shining pockets to my island: I'm pretty good.

Bummer

I've lost the taste for it, this life,
and lost my dear friends plus all joy;
I've lost my pride even: the dram
of diesel running my engine.

I'd had a pretty good feeling
I'd been companionable
until at last I understood
and was disgusted with myself.

It goes on and on, anyway,
without dread a few steps behind
who finishes anything?

God calls, and we ought to pick up.
My only asset in this world
is to have had recently wept.

from the French of Alfred De Musset

The Butcher

It is the coldest noon in twenty years.
Outside deer are nowhere to be seen and inside
the radio spectrum fills up with sorrowful little packets of data.
Wasn't there a hart at the window yesterday, he thinks,
weren't there huge antlers and if so what if
anything is there to be said of the unanswerable
phone ringing as it's been ringing lately
and of the village the blue of snow desiccated coconut of snow
and there on the fold up table folded out for once
the bowl of raisins she has eaten none of
for fear of unsettling her veil, today of all todays
and dawn coming so late last night it resembled mercy
until at last it came, resembling cruelty.
And what is there to say of all the hands and wrists
and forearms and the men shaking them and their regrets
into his palms like hucksters shilling counterfeits
and later over whiskey nodding stories of times
they were right and other men were wrong
and how the pub was closed for an hour as a mark of respect
and chimney smoke over the village as though it was coffee cooling.
What is there to do with the sick pigeon sanctuaried against the
    woodpile
the beech tree was before the lightning brought it down which he
    claimed
with his beech-handled axe before the rest of town got wind of it
which he and the boy tramped back to the house with that last
    time.
And what can be left to say about the snow globe
in which all of this happens without taking away from the butcher
who must get to work grief or no grief if his neighbours are to eat

who must begin his work of opening up the way he will the
        newspaper
the coldest winter in twenty years
goes the headline and somewhere under the canopy
of the woods goes deer shattering themselves against one another
with an architecture of golden blood and a rage they can't express.

A Quarter Mile of Voices

A loaf steals a bread of starving man
to feed his long-necked elegant children,
to feed his long-necked elegant wife
my carabiner, my love
whose tender, brittle kiss on the cheek
sleeps in the old van's passenger seat
with the telescopic ladder and the bolt cutters
since bread is sometimes telephone wires
and what's fifty volts between friends,
what's a shiver of headlights on the roadside,
what's a great big outlaw country music moon.

Divine a price, black marketeer, for copper
enchanted with suspended conversations.
Abandoned building site and handshake me,
thimblerig and swindle me.
On the first night, they observed the feast of
    Yes but McCarthy died in 1957.
On the second night, they observed the feast of
    hotel bar, Thursday, eight o'clock.
On the third night, they observed the feast of
    I can't stand it, his eyes.

O,

Earl Strickland I dislike you quite a lot
and it's not because you are a Gemini.

You skulk up to the table like a Gemini,
like a little god of diligence, fury,

and full-body English nine-ball breaks
but it's not really even that.

It's not the wrap-around sports sunglasses
or the pernickety quiver of break and game cues,

and hey, a belly is not unbecoming
for certain gentlemen of a certain age.

It's not the bristled trapezium
of your unmodish blond moustache,

it's not the cyan Lycra billiard glove,
chichi in the extreme, and less still

that weighted arm band fixed around your bicep
as an amulet or periapt. Whatever.

Earl, yours is a game for one played by two:
one of whom is you and the other, you.

From those regional pool halls eye-watering
with smoke, a bad moon often on the rise,

to the Riviera Hotel and Casino, Nevada
and the 8-ball Open sponsored by Camel—

you play in a long off-beat.
A gold tooth rattles down a drainpipe.

Earl Strickland I dislike you quite a lot
and not because you shellacked Stephen Hendry.

It's not the cues of cocobolo or rosewood
or who knows, the drawn and dressed neck and spine of a
        whooper swan

wrapped with stacked leather or Irish linen,
or the cotton you picked for pool money

on the farm in Roseboro, North Carolina;
and its tobacco, and its fat striped watermelons

rolling in the back of a pick-up truck
at angles you could, as a child, calculate.

Earl Strickland I dislike you quite a lot
for the junk of your regalia and your sneer.

Earl Strickland I dislike you quite a lot
for the beauty you achieve when beauty

is never your intention.
Earl Strickland, make like Pangaea and break.

Make like some ancient stage magician
who has cinched the trick so many times

he has finally forgotten how and when
the sleight of hand happens—

for whom it is a mystery the moment
a white handkerchief turns into a dove.

For the Birds

From the mountain the glittering city,
the lough a field of static, the mountain
tumorous with gold or said to be,
the bittering meadow odour of animals.
From the mountain, its path:
bolt-cutters to fault the telephone alarm
and showing flocks of arrows, confronted deer
in madder-bordered glowing pastures,
an Anatolian carpet for the barbed wire fences.
The deer have your eyes, Cheryl, the moonlight your clavicle.
It's practically always the anniversary of something terrible:
twenty-six years since skaters took to the thawing lake;
one-hundred-and-twenty-one since the clerk and his sweetheart
and a revolver honoured their pact on the north-eastern slope
where a Barnum of topical forest, tire-swings and wood chip
adjoins the microtonal panic of the aviary
where soon, and never coming back,
flying things fly towards their context.

Daydream of the Jacket

My new vintage Houndstooth jacket was catching eyes
in the aisles of the supermarket. I felt like someone else:
an older man perhaps, a taller man, a man without a beard
and when I saw myself reflected in the freezer glass, I was.

I felt I had known myself for many years up to this point.
I stood like the coy in decoy in the quiet supermarket
between the frozen raspberries and the shredded suet
when my neighbour Mrs Carmichael rounded the corner.

Coconut oil, coconut milk, desiccated coconut:
her basket was a who's who of coconut.
I supposed she was cooking something with coconut
though Mr Carmichael had always been the one to shop.

Together at the checkout, she too admired my jacket
and its unimpeachable stitches. This was when
I remembered there had been rain on our wedding day,
burgundy leather in the big car, a rear window, my parents –

that into my jacket I slipped this morning a shopping list
that for all my life I was sure I was someone younger.
Then she said, you are my husband aren't you, I am, I said
and went home, and since we kept canaries, fed the canaries.

So it is,

i.m. Ciaran Carson

a detail of wind turbines combs the oakish hills
and fields gorse-limned, fallow, or dazzled with eyebright.

These craftless rotors transform the invisible
into the intangible: the good breeze of breath

becomes the lamplight farmers study journals by;
the pall of streetlights drawing towards the city;

the dreadful candle of the crematorium.
I know the road's every inch; its urgent camber

and final curve at which the country falls away,
where like a diorama of itself, Belfast

emerges shining among its accoutrements
of history, mystery, industry, river.

If the office of Lagander is obsolete,
no matter—unaccounted for bails of linen

plugs of tobacco, barrels of barley and hops
remain unaccounted for, well-settled by now,

sunk into the strata of centuries of silt
where above, the river, old ornithomancer,

interprets its future from cascades of starlings,
big moons, and how many years ago now?—ourselves

smoking cigarettes on a rickety gangplank
after a spell of your verse on the long-moored barge.

Was that the night Stephen and me skippered the boat
as far as the railway bridge after a few beers

coursing at a blistering half a knot an hour,
safely chaperoned by its registered keeper

who knew his starboard from his sherry, and took steer,
and figure-of-eighted us between the columns

and puffed the little skiff back to its mothership?
Those nights of Brí and Rachel's hospitality,

of poems from Wayne and Andy and Leontia
Sophie, Sam, Jack, Sinéad in the Galley Café,

the barge sweltered like a greenhouse and rocked in storms.
Once, you accepted Żubrówka, whose long blade

of bison grass goes aquiver with its measures
and our talk turned to tempers of accordions;

the proper box and the *no no no* piano
whose big breath and bellows I was enamoured of,

whose ranks and banks of reeds, switches, rods and buttons
are engineered for the alchemy we're after—

to return the unvibrating air vibrating.

*

Nights our odd spring the ISS darts past Derry,
a dash of cirrus hangs over the cathedral,

a teenager runs modes and pentatonic scales
in his bedroom, and otherwise, the world is still.

The *X-Files* illuminates the moon-hours I keep.
O to love anything the way Mulder loves truth!

amid an enmity of beasts and shapeshifters,
extra-terrestrials and worse: terrestrials,

cover ups, undercover investigators,
and a supernaturally corrupt government.

And it turns out, according to the OED
that a *muld* may well be a tribute of millet

less suited to Apollo than to Mercury,
god of eloquence, translator of souls, keeper

of boundaries and thresholds; god of the Falls Road
you might allow, *hence, any kind of enclosed thing*.

I miss those afternoons of etymology
in small back rooms both dishabille and elegant,

digressing from Donaghadee to ecstasy;
and thence the country and western singing contest

you won in either North or South Carolina.
What American pool players mean by *English*

is side spin, and it's all metaphor anyhow,
so much carrying across: Turnbull and his horse

the insurmountable distances between thing
and thingnified; between sing and sound and silence;

the key, the quay, the qui, the river and the land
reclaimed from mud-stuck estuarial floodplains.

Belfast is yours by nature, mine through affection,
and sometimes your cut of Donegal tweed and hat

would appear beyond me towards Rosemary Street
and linger at the window of the jeweller's

or slip out of view into Pottinger's Entry
or Joy's Entry, or the long decay of North Street

and the ruin of its arson-stricken arcade:
its bookshop's proprietor eating fish and chips

from *The Mirror*, an atmosphere of vinegar;
its surly and prohibitive head shop owner,

his embarrassment of paraphernalia;
the Arcadia café lost by now to myth.

From the university, I watched smoke pillar
as the bank buildings burned the town to a standstill.

Belfast became again a city of side streets.

*

Flocks of whirr and harry, a surveillance of drones
over and above the cordon's jurisdiction.

A spark thrown out by the quirk of a bad circuit
on the roof, it happens, and the fire grows legs

and downstairs tries on every outfit in the shop.
Of fast fashion's soft furnishings, nothing remains;

warped beams and girders skew like an asterisk drunk
but the sandstone stonework of balustrades and urns

survives, a little blackened, flanking the stopped clock.
The sky of your last good summer is filled with smoke.

The bad brigade of cells was working on you then
or at least was knotting its tie in the mirror

while fire crews cooled the city with its river
and all routes North-South may not include the centre.

By the time the good doctor had shaken his head
the wreck of the building was bolstered with scaffolds—

a pyramid of shipping containers painted
safety yellow made a docklands of Castle Street

as though a century is nothing, and some ship
clinkered and straked and riveted and fitted out

were to be loaded with potatoes and coffee,
tea and oranges and opium and toothpaste,

love letters and a handful of grand pianos
whose fortunes as flotsam and lagan were not yet

set in stone, who might yet survive translation west
and rendition Irish airs to America

whose cities now bristle under cities of smoke;
whose people are murdered in the street by the state;

whose atmosphere vibrates with harmonies of rage
and it's not as if we're far beyond it ourselves:

locals only howl locals only in moonlight,
brushes dripping with white paint, bullets in the mail.

Is to love its language and music and promise
to be complicit in its terror—I don't know.

Arpeggios of fiddles and tuning guitars—
some decades ago a Country and Western star,

whose destiny even then held this elegy,
draws a sip of moonshine from a brown paper bag,

shrugs off his jacket, rolls his sleeves, loosens his tie,
and sings an aisling, or 'The Wild Colonial Boy',

and vanishes in the applause and the stage lights.

*

Near the clinic my father told me a story.
We're on the back lanes, winding between barley fields,

lean, gambolling lambs and the new developments;
a method of hidden dips and salient bends.

He says these roads aren't by accident, but design,
that dragging its burden of produce or timber

a horse thinks of every turn as the final turn
for home, that a horizon is too much to bear.

He says I should remember this for a poem.
It's true enough—I can feel the ache in my hooves,

tension burning its omens into my haunches.
There's sadness in my eyes and sadness in my eyes.

On the hills of the world, turbines turn their great torques;
the breath the wind is made of is some part still yours.

What's poetry but the art of failing to make
a moment happened once forever happen twice?

Mulder won't make it for this toast to you tonight—
a government of fiction governs by fiction.

Of the Polish vodka, one enthusiast says
long finish, ending up on grass and fresh flowers.

The still lifes I love, and they are unbearable.
Once, during those months of *La Vita Nuova,*

somehow having fetched another fetch of yourself
word rumoured you back at the head of the table.

We ran from small back rooms and stairways to witness,
from the corridor's door's arrow-slit window, you

glowing, poisoned, under a new, white fuzz of hair
smiling as a new poem found its way forward.

It's there I see you last, all of us jostling
to say, for the last time, hello to the master.

The Farset, culverted, disappears underground.
The Lagan bears its sunk cargo, its many turns,

in order to remain entirely itself;
as you're wont to say, maestro, it is what it is.

However the city's missing middle's remade,
the detour's handsomer by far than the main road

which leads us here, anyway: to the parting glass;
to dawn or something like it showing up on time;

to the sad and sweet laying down of instruments;
to the blink that changes last night into today

where light falls on nothing finer than two fried eggs.

NOTES

'Siamese Dream for the Cloths of Heaven: A Collaboration' was composed in collaboration with Georgie Hyde-Lees (1892–1968), who revealed to me the identity of one of her many 'communicators' and the influence of The Smashing Pumpkins on the poetry of W. B. Yeats.

The poems in Part II reference lyrics from The Smashing Pumpkins' *Siamese Dream*. '4:58' quotes from 'Cherub Rock'; '3:41' from 'Quiet'; '3:19' from 'Today'; '6:57' from 'Hummer'; '4:06' from 'Rocket'; '3:17' from 'Disarm'; '5:13' from 'Geek USA'; '4:28' from 'Spaceboy'; '8:43' from 'Silverfuck'; '1:38' from 'Sweet Sweet'; '3:20' from Luna; ' ' from 'Silverfuck', all written by Billy Corgan. '6:39' quotes from 'Soma', '5:50' from 'Mayonnaise', both written by Billy Corgan and James Iha.

'For Gomez' is in affectionate memory of Raúl Julia (1940–94).

'From *The Beasley Contract Bridge System, 1935*' is made up of phrases taken from *The Beasley Contract Bridge System* by Lt-Col H. M. Beasley, which was published in 1935.

'Bummer' is a translation of 'Tristesse' by Alfred De Musset (1810–57).

ACKNOWLEDGEMENTS

I'm grateful to the editors of the following publications in which some poems, or versions of them, first appeared:

Agenda, Bath Magg, Copper Nickel, Cordite Poetry Review, The Cormorant, The Future Always Makes Me So Thirsty: New Poets from the North of Ireland, Granta, Islands are But Mountains, POETRY, Poetry Ireland Review, Southword, The Tangerine, The Telegraph, Virginia Quarterly Review.

Thanks to Tracy Bohan and the Wylie Agency, and to Maria Bedford and everyone at Penguin. Thank you to friends and colleagues and students at the Seamus Heaney Centre at Queen's University, Belfast, and to Damian Smyth and the Arts Council of Northern Ireland.

Thank you to Dane Holt and Padraig Regan for their advice and friendship, and to Michael Nolan, Scott McKendry and Wayne Miller.

Love to Bríd, always.